4 WEEKS

# The Spanish in AMERICA

by
LINDA THOMPSON

Rourke
Publishing LLC
Vero Beach, Florida 32964

www.rourkepublishing.com

**PHOTO CREDITS:**
Bonsal, Stephen, *Edward Fitzgerald Beale*, 1912: page 32; Courtesy Library of Congress, Edward S. Curtis Collection: pages 13, 18; Courtesy Library of Congress, Prints and Photographs Division: Title Page, pages 5, 6, 7, 9, 14, 15, 20, 21, 27, 28, 34, 37, 39, 40, 41; Courtesy Library of Congress, Rare Books and Special Collections Division: pages 25, 33; Courtesy NASA: page 31; Courtesy National Oceanic and Atmospheric Administration: pages 4, 35, 43; Courtesy National Parks Service: page 12; Courtesy Rohm Padilla: pages 26, 32, 42; Courtesy Charles Reasoner: pages 10, 22, 23; Courtesy U.S. Army, Center of Military History: pages 19, 29.

**SPECIAL NOTE:** Further information about glossary terms in bold in the text can be found on page 46. More information about people's names shown in the text in bold can be found on page 47.

**DESIGN: ROHM PADILLA**
**LAYOUT/PRODUCTION: LUCY PADILLA**

**Library of Congress Cataloging-in-Publication Data**

Library of Congress Cataloging-in-Publication Data

Thompson, Linda, 1941-
    The Spanish in America / Linda Thompson.
       p. cm. -- (The expansion of America II)
    Includes bibliographical references (p.   ) and index.
    ISBN 1-59515-514-7 (hardcover : alk. paper)
    1. Spaniards--America--History--Juvenile literature.  2. America
--Discovery and exploration--Spanish--Juvenile literature.  3. America
--History--To 1810--Juvenile literature.  4. Spain--Colonies--America
--History--Juvenile literature.    I. Title. II. Series: Thompson,
Linda,
    1941-   . Expansion of America II.
    E29.S65T48 2006
    973'.0461--dc22

2005015373

**TITLE PAGE IMAGE**
Fort St. Augustine, Florida

# TABLE OF CONTENTS

# Chapter I: **LA FLORIDA**

The first European attempt at a settlement in what became the United States was made in 1526—only 34 years after **Christopher Columbus** first landed in the New World. This was **San Miguel de Gualdape**, founded by Spain on North America's Atlantic coast. It happened nearly 60 years before the founding of **Roanoke**, which is often considered the first settlement in North America.

A marker in Hispaniola near the area of Columbus's landing

Like Roanoke, San Miguel de Gualdape was doomed to fail. The dream of a Spanish lawyer named **Lucas Vásquez de Ayllón**, the outpost lasted only two months. Indian attacks, disease, their leader's death, and conflict with each other proved too much for these settlers as they struggled to exist on the coast of what is now Georgia or southern South Carolina. Of the 500 people who sailed from the settlement of Santo Domingo in the **West Indies**, only 150 survived to return.

After that failure, Spain made several more attempts at establishing a foothold on the Florida coast and finally succeeded. St. Augustine, Florida, about 40 miles (64 km) south of today's Jacksonville, is the oldest permanent European settlement in the United States. It was founded as **San Augustín** on September 8, 1565. The founder, **Pedro Menéndez de Avilés**, claimed this sheltered harbor and all of the land called "La Florida" in the name of his king, **Felipe II**.

Pedro Menéndez de Avilés

5

## THE NAME OF "LA FLORIDA"

**Juan Ponce de León** first saw Florida shores on April 2, 1513. Easter was coming so he named the land "Pascua Florida," or Floral Easter. It became known as "La Florida" [Flor-EE-da]. No written records exist to confirm the popular legend that Ponce was searching for a "fountain of youth."

Juan Ponce de León

A carving showing a Spanish priest and Native Americans planting a cross

All of Spain's explorations and early colonizing were linked to spreading the **Roman Catholic** faith. The Spanish king and **conquistadors** saw themselves as agents of the Catholic Church in America, viewing other **sects** as a threat to the "true religion." They believed that having left the Catholic Church, Protestants were "guilty of rebellion" and could "expect no mercy," as Felipe II had written.

These beliefs help explain the cruel behavior of many of the early explorers, including Christopher Columbus. Many Europeans believed that **Native Americans** held the wrong ideas about religion, which needed to be changed.

Columbus greeted by Arawak Native Americans. His men plant a cross in the background.

On **Hispaniola**, the West Indies island Columbus first **colonized**, slavery, harsh punishment, and European diseases wiped out 200,000 of the 250,000 **Arawak** Native Americans within 20 years.

Other explorers and settlers followed the example set by Columbus. These included **Hernán Cortés** in Mexico, **Francisco Pizarro** in Peru, English settlers in Virginia and Massachusetts, and Dutch colonists in New York. The Spaniards were mainly searching for "God, Gold, and Glory." That meant **converting** Native Americans to Catholicism, finding gold and silver to take back to their king, and winning fame and honor for themselves. But another very important goal was finding land for people to live on.

Between 1519 and 1521 Hernán Cortés was defeating the **Aztec** empire in what is now Mexico. He founded a colony there, **Nueva España** ("New Spain"), which lasted 300 years. By 1531 Francisco Pizarro had begun to conquer the **Inca** empire in present-day Peru. Within a few years, Mexico and Peru, with their rich deposits of gold and silver, were major sources of Spanish wealth and power in the New World.

As time passed, it was necessary to build more **fortresses** and towns in La Florida. From the 1550s on, French pirates raided Spanish ships loaded with gold and silver. Soon English pirates, such as **Sir Francis Drake**, were doing the same. The waters off Florida and the West Indies were favorite **marauding** spots.

An Aztec pyramid in Mexico

Another reason for Spain to build up its defenses had to do with the religious **conversion** of Native Americans. Menéndez had first brought **missionaries** in 1565. Within a few years, Spain had built missions and small forts to protect them around the tip of Florida to the Gulf Coast. In 1573, a royal proclamation from the king gave missionaries an important role in exploring and settling new lands. **Franciscan** priests arrived to staff the missions and baptized thousands of Indians.

Francisco Pizarro

In the early 1600s, Spain was considering abandoning La Florida, but the missionaries argued that the converts needed their spiritual leadership. They appealed to **Felipe III** and convinced him not to leave.

## SPANISH LAST NAMES

Spanish last names usually consist of the father's last name followed by the mother's last name. As a shortened form, only the father's last name is used. Therefore, Pedro Menéndez de Avilés is known as "Menéndez." There are exceptions to this rule. For example, Francisco Vásquez de Coronado is known as "Coronado," his mother's name.

The adventure of **Álvar Nuñez Cabeza de Vaca** shows the difficulties Spain faced in its early colonizing attempts. Cabeza de Vaca accompanied **Pánfilo de Narváez**, who had permission from the king to settle lands along the coast of the **Gulf of Mexico**. In 1528 they landed south of Tampa Bay with about 390 men.

Álvar Nuñez Cabeza de Vaca underwent great changes on his journey.

By April 1529 only 14 men remained. None would have survived except that Cabeza de Vaca had learned the art of herbal healing, becoming known among the Indians as a medicine man. The small party traveled westward with a growing escort of Indians. They probably passed through land that is now southern New Mexico and Arizona.

In the spring of 1536, Cabeza de Vaca and three survivors walked into a village on Mexico's Pacific coast! Spaniards hunting for slaves to work in Mexico's silver mines were astounded to see four nearly naked men, one black and the others a deep bronze, arrive with a large group of Native American followers. The four continued on to Mexico City. They had come more than 3,500 miles (5,633 km) in eight years!

Cabeza de Vaca wrote reports of his astonishing adventure. He described people living in villages in the land he had walked through, some with houses four or five stories high. These people practiced farming and traded in **emeralds**, **turquoise** stones, and buffalo robes. His stories attracted the attention of two powerful men in Mexico City, Hernán Cortés and the **viceroy**, or governor, **Antonio de Mendoza**. They would soon launch new expeditions to explore and settle the interior of North America.

# Chapter II: **NUEVO MÉXICO**

Besides Florida, Spain's major foothold in North America for 200 years was New Mexico. Like Florida, New Mexico was considered much larger than the present state of that name, reaching into areas that are now Arizona, Nevada, Utah, Colorado, and other states. It was a made-up tale of golden cities that distracted every explorer of New Mexico well into the 17th century. Searching for these cities kept the Spaniards moving on rather than settling down.

Coronado National Memorial, Arizona

Inspired by Cabeza de Vaca's reports, Antonio de Mendoza wanted to expand his **domain** north of Mexico. He could not convince Cabeza de Vaca or the other two Spaniards to return as guides, so he purchased a black slave, **Esteban**, to take part in an expedition headed by **Francisco Vásquez de Coronado** in 1540.

In preparation for Coronado's journey, Mendoza sent Esteban with a party led by a Franciscan **friar**, **Marcos de Niza**. Within a year, Father Marcos returned with stories of rich kingdoms with jewel-covered temples and exotic animals such as camels and elephants. He called this land "the **Seven Cities of Cíbola**." His stories encouraged Mendoza to speed up plans for the Coronado expedition.

## THE FATE OF ESTEBAN

Father Marcos had Esteban, the black slave, scout ahead with several hundred Natives. Esteban sent back a Native American with a white cross whenever he found something important. After Esteban sent back a very large cross, he was not heard from again. Later, it was learned that **Zuni** Indians had killed him. The Zuni mud villages were probably the "Seven Cities of Cíbola" that Father Marcos described, although Marcos most likely had not seen them himself.

Terraced houses of Zuni Pueblo

Landing of de Soto in Florida

Before Coronado departed, another conquistador sailed from the West Indies to explore land west of Florida. **Hernando Méndez de Soto y Gutiérrez Cardeñosa** had permission to explore and settle all of Florida. He and other Spaniards believed that "La Florida" stretched west to Mexico and north perhaps as far as Canada. With 600 men, de Soto marched across what is now the southeastern United States. In 1542, he became ill and died. Four months later, when his troops returned to Mexico, only half of them were still alive.

## THE DEVASTATION CAUSED BY DE SOTO

De Soto passed through a region with large populations of Native Americans. His men were the only outsiders to see large populations of Apalachee, Cofitachequi, **Coosa**, **Tascaloosa**, and similar tribes living in prosperity before European diseases destroyed them. Many Native Americans fought the intruders, who took slaves, food, and supplies by force. Thousands of Native Americans died after the Spaniards had passed through because they had no **immunity** to diseases such as **typhus**, **typhoid**, **smallpox**, and **measles**.

In early 1540, Coronado left Mexico and passed through what is now southern Arizona. When he reached the Zuni villages, he was disappointed to see two-story mud buildings rather than the fabled Cíbola. Coronado read the Zuni the **requerimiento**, a strange ceremony Spanish conquerors had to perform in America. It revealed to the inhabitants that God and the **Pope** had given the Americas to the king of Spain. Native Americans were ordered to submit to this authority and to agree to convert to Catholicism. If they refused, the Spaniards said, "we shall forcefully enter your country and make war against you in all ways."

Coronado leading his men

## THE RIO GRANDE PUEBLOS

Early Spanish explorers came upon more than 100 settlements along the Rio Grande River and called them "pueblos," meaning "villages." They were solidly built mud buildings, often two or three stories high, with central plazas. The people grew corn, squash, beans, and cotton; hunted game; and gathered wild plants to eat. They spoke at least nine different languages and had trade networks over long distances.

It is unlikely that the Zuni and other Native American groups understood this statement read to them in a foreign language. The Zuni resisted, firing arrows at the intruders. But Coronado took the village by force and made it his headquarters. He sent scouting parties in several directions. Some of his men scouted the Rio Grande River valley, visiting more than 100 **pueblos** between present-day Taos and Albuquerque, New Mexico, and eastward to **Pecos**, one of the largest of the pueblos.

Taos Pueblo, one of many along the Rio Grande

Meanwhile, Viceroy Mendoza had become interested in the Pacific coast. He commissioned another Spaniard, **Juan Rodríguez Cabrillo**, to seek a water passage that might link the Atlantic and Pacific oceans. Cabrillo left Mexico's western coast in 1542, sailing north. Cabrillo and his men explored 1,200 miles (1,930 km) of the **Baja California** and **Alta California** coastline, giving Spain a claim to the entire Pacific coast of North America. But Spain did not begin to colonize California for another 225 years.

New Mexico's first permanent European settlement came about in 1598. **Juan Oñate y Salazar** had been named governor and **adelantado**, as well as captain-general, of all of New Mexico. He set out with about 500 people, determined to form a colony. About 25 miles (40 km) from present El Paso, Texas, Oñate formally claimed the land for King Felipe II and himself.

## THE OTHER FIRST THANKSGIVING

Near El Paso, Oñate's group rested for a week. The local Native Americans, whom they called **Mansos**, brought great quantities of fish in exchange for clothing and gifts. The feast that followed—23 years before the more famous event at Plymouth Rock—is celebrated in El Paso as the first Thanksgiving in the United States.

In July 1598 Oñate established his first capital at a pueblo named Okhe, which he called San Juan de los Caballeros. Today this is San Juan Pueblo, north of Santa Fe. After a couple of months he moved across the river to Yungé pueblo, which Oñate named San Gabriel. From these bases, Franciscan friars spread out along the Rio Grande and began the process of conversion. At each pueblo Oñate read the requerimiento, later reporting to the king that all pueblo leaders had agreed to become subjects of Spain.

San Juan Pueblo

Oñate was often away on explorations and neglected San Gabriel. Lacking leadership, many of his colonists returned to Mexico. For this reason, and also his mistreatment of Native Ameicans, the king ordered that Oñate be replaced. The king considered abandoning New Mexico because, like Florida, it was a drain on the treasury. But in 1608, the Franciscan friars convinced the king to allow them to continue their **ministry** to the Native Ameicans. By 1629 Spain had more than 25 missions in New Mexico, with 50 priests and more than 60,000 baptized Native Ameicans practicing Christianity.

## THE FOUNDING OF SANTA FE

Some of Oñate's settlers moved south from San Gabriel to what is now Santa Fe, New Mexico. In 1610, Oñate's successor, **Pedro de Peralta**, named it the "Villa Real de Santa Fe." Santa Fe is the oldest capital city in the United States.

Santa Fe in the 1800s

During the 1600s fewer than 2,000 Spaniards lived in Florida and probably fewer than 3,000 in New Mexico. But though they were few, Spaniards began to influence the large Native American populations in many ways. Native Americans did not give up their religions, but combined their beliefs with those taught by the missionaries. Native Americans also learned about cattle, horses and mules, sheep and goats, pigs, the plow, and wheat, which—unlike corn—could be grown in the winter. They learned to read and write Spanish, became blacksmiths and carpenters, and adopted new ways of weaving and cooking. The Spanish also learned from the Native Americans, and the blending of the two cultures created a unique way of life that endures today, especially in the Southwest.

Feast day at San Estevan del Rey Mission, Acoma Pueblo, New Mexico

# Chapter III: **REVOLT AND RECONQUEST**

In both Florida and New Mexico, Spanish rule began to collapse in the late 17th century. One reason was that both church and government forced Native Americans to work hard without pay. Spaniards depended on Native American labor for their well being. They had to build missions, farm fields, produce blankets and cloth, and otherwise contribute to the settlement's earnings. They were also forced to travel to areas where **nomadic** tribes held trade fairs. They had to **barter** for bison hides and deerskins and bring them back.

Inside a Native American blacksmith shop, Zuni Pueblo

Timucuan Indians being forced to search for gold in Florida

In Florida, Native Americans struggled to build and supply more than 30 missions, growing food, cotton, and tobacco for the friars. They were forced to work on public projects; they repaired roads, built bridges, operated ferry services, unloaded ships, and accompanied wagon trains. They were paid little or nothing for these services. Some soldiers and settlers illegally forced Native Americans to work for them personally. An especially humiliating job was to serve as a human pack animal, hauling cargo.

Native Americans also suffered from **drought** and disease. In 1640, smallpox killed 3,000 Natives in New Mexico, nearly 10 percent of the entire pueblo population. Additional epidemics occurred in the 1660s. From 1667 to 1672, a lack of rain caused widespread starvation, with no crops harvested between 1665 and 1668. All of these forces led to an amazing event in 1680 called "the Pueblo Revolt."

About 30,000 Pueblo Indians lived in New Mexico, greatly outnumbering the 2,300 Spaniards. A San Juan Native named **Popé** led a rebellion involving some 17,000 Indians. Planning the revolt and keeping it secret was a remarkable accomplishment because the Pueblo people spoke different languages and lived in more than two dozen villages spread over several hundred miles. Popé managed to unite most of the other pueblos against the Spaniards. Some neighboring **Apaches**, who resented the colonists' practice of enslaving their people, also joined in.

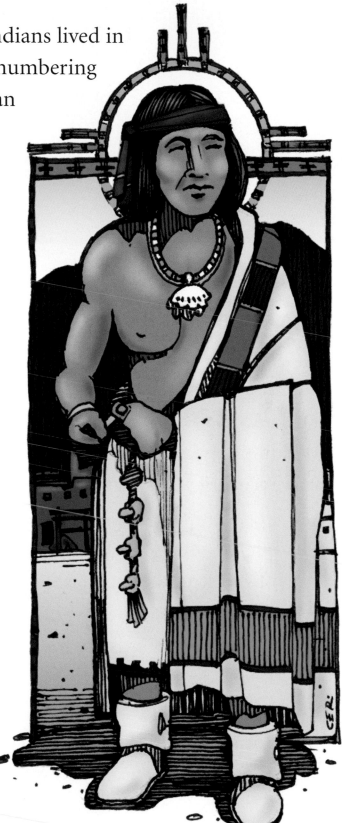

Pueblo revolt leader Popé

The first church at Taos Pueblo was destroyed in the Pueblo Revolt. After being rebuilt in 1706, it was ruined again in 1847 by the U.S. military.

On August 9, 1680, Native Americans in Taos and San Juan began burning and looting churches and homes. Spanish arms and livestock were seized. Popé ordered every Catholic object destroyed because Native Americans were to return to their old religions. Baptisms were to be reversed. The revolt spread to the south, as well as to Zuni on the west and the Hopi villages in the north. Within a few days all of the missions had been destroyed, with 21 missionaries and nearly 400 **colonists** killed.

In 1680 Spain also began to lose power in La Florida. Eager to control the fur trade and the coastline, English settlers in Carolina allied with Native American tribes to drive out the Spaniards. By the end of 1706, they had wiped out all Florida missions except those near San Augustín. As in New Mexico, large numbers of Native Americans joined in the attacks and renounced Christianity. Unlike what happened in New Mexico, however, Spain would not be able to reconquer its Florida colony.

The flight of Spanish colonists to El Paso prompted the first mission building in what is now Texas. More than 300 Native Americans had fled with the Spaniards needed homes. In 1682 Franciscans founded several missions there, as well as in east Texas. They were most successful in the area of what is now San Antonio. The San Antonio de Valero mission, begun in 1718, would later become famous as "The Alamo." A **presidio**, or fort, was added to protect the mission. To populate San Antonio, Spain brought immigrants from its Canary Island colony, off the coast of northern Africa.

Native Americans at a Spanish mission

By this time, the Spanish had retaken New Mexico. Spain sent a new commander to El Paso, **Diego de Vargas Zapata Luján y Ponce de León**. In 1692 Vargas took a small force (fewer than 200 soldiers and several missionaries) up the Rio Grande with a daring strategy. When he reached a pueblo, instead of attacking with guns he had his soldiers sing hymns and pray. With a **fanfare** of trumpets and drums, he **pacified** the Natives of 23 pueblos and raised the Spanish flag. Returning to El Paso in December, he began to prepare for the reconquest.

Diego de Vargas Zapata Luján y Ponce de León

In the fall of 1693, Vargas triumphantly led about 800 people back to New Mexico, but many Native Americans had changed their minds. The Spaniards spent a year fighting up and down the Rio Grande. As missions were rebuilt, Native Americans resisted, killing five more Franciscans in 1696. Gradually, however, the pueblos were brought under control except for the Hopi, who never did submit to the reconquest.

# Chapter IV: LOSING AMERICA

The 18th century saw Spain expanding into new regions of America as well as giving up land to its rivals. During this century, Spain's most important colonization efforts took place in California.

Spain sided with France in the **French and Indian War** (known as the Seven Years' War in Europe). France lost the war and signed the Treaty of Paris of 1763, which forced Spain to give La Florida to England. The English changed San Augustín's name to St. Augustine.

A battle during the French and Indian War, 1755

# THE BACK AND FORTH OF FLORIDA

After Spain established Pensacola in 1698, it became the center of life in western Florida. When England acquired La Florida in 1763, the country divided it into two provinces, East Florida and West Florida. After the American Revolution, both Floridas were given back to Spain. Then, in 1819, the United States bought all of Florida for $5 million and made it a territory in 1821.

---

But Spain had won another prize—the vast region of Louisiana! France had transferred ownership in a secret treaty in 1762 to avoid losing it to England. Spain thought Louisiana would serve as a **buffer**, helping protect its western colonies, especially Nueva España.

The siege of Pensacola. Spanish troops in the foreground force the surrender of the British garrison.

Like the English, however, the French had sold arms to Native Americans—something that Spain had forbidden its settlers and traders to do. In Texas, **Comanches** and their allies, armed by the French, forced the abandonment of missions and presidios. Around San Antonio, the missions succeeded but they never drew more than a few hundred converts. Without Native

José de Galvez

American labor, the settlers did their own farming and ranching. These settlers were also few, with only about 1,200 living in the area in 1760.

With both France and England gaining ground, Spain increased its defenses across the frontier. In 1769, King **Carlos III** turned his attention to California. He sent **José de Gálvez** to make recommendations. Gálvez was especially interested in the northern frontier, where English and Russian fur traders operated. He suggested building missions and presidios from San Diego to Monterey Bay.

A statue in California of Junípero Serra

The Franciscan friar responsible for beginning to build Spanish missions in "New California" was **Junípero Serra**. This 55-year-old friar became one of the best known priests in American history. In 1769, he built the first of 21 missions, San Diego de Álcala. Meanwhile, Captain **Gaspar de Portolá** took 60 men by foot from San Diego to seek a trail for the friars to follow. He missed Monterey Bay and instead discovered San Francisco Bay. A year later, he reached Monterey and built a presidio with a mission attached. In 1777 Monterey was named the capital of New California.

The biggest challenge in California was getting food and supplies to the settlements. Some ships were wrecked in storms while men waiting on the coast died of **scurvy** and hunger. Gálvez understood that if the missions were to flourish, he would have to find a dependable overland route and bring families, single women, livestock, and supplies from Sonora, a Mexican province south of Arizona.

In January 1774, Captain **Juan Bautista de Anza** left Sonora with 34 men to search for an overland route to the California coast. They crossed the Colorado River and continued to Monterey. In 1775, Anza led a group of 240 men and women over this route. Some settled in Monterey, while others moved north to become the first San Francisco colonists.

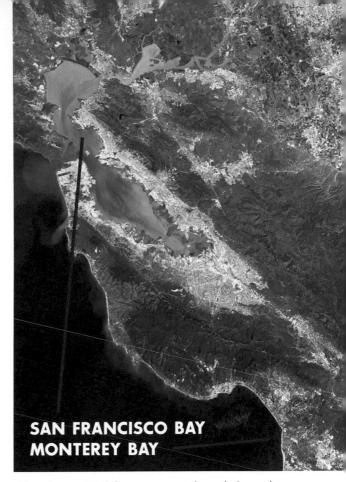

SAN FRANCISCO BAY
MONTEREY BAY

Northern California coastline (above).
San Francisco in the 1800s (below)

In 1781, however, Yuma Indians closed the Colorado River crossing and it stayed closed for 40 years. Fortunately, mission farming had become successful within the few years that the land route had been open. After 1781, Spanish settlements in California depended on food that the missions produced or brought from Mexico once or twice a year by ship.

By the time Serra died in 1784, nine missions had been built in a 550-mile (885-km) long chain. Under his **successors**, 11 more were built. More than 21,000 Native Americans lived at the missions. The last mission, San Francisco Solano (in the town of Sonoma), was not built until 1823, after Mexico had won its independence from Spain.

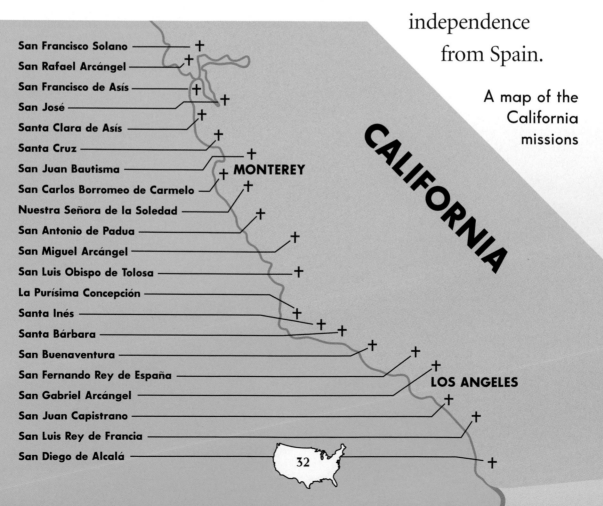

A map of the California missions

San Francisco Solano
San Rafael Arcángel
San Francisco de Asís
San José
Santa Clara de Asís
Santa Cruz
San Juan Bautisma
San Carlos Borromeo de Carmelo
Nuestra Señora de la Soledad
San Antonio de Padua
San Miguel Arcángel
San Luis Obispo de Tolosa
La Purísima Concepción
Santa Inés
Santa Bárbara
San Buenaventura
San Fernando Rey de España
San Gabriel Arcángel
San Juan Capistrano
San Luis Rey de Francia
San Diego de Alcalá

MONTEREY

CALIFORNIA

LOS ANGELES

Mestizos washing clothes and carrying water in California

## THE CALIFORNIOS

By 1800, there were about 1,800 Hispanic people in Alta California. These included Spaniards, **criollos**, and **mestizos**. All of them lived along the 500-mile (805-km) coastal region between San Diego and San Francisco. Most lived in California's three towns (Los Angeles, San Jose, and Branciforte—which became Santa Cruz) or near one of the four military presidios: San Diego, Santa Barbara, Monterey, and San Francisco.

A major event in 1783 set the stage for the closing years of Spain's North American empire. The United States of America was born! Through its alliance with France, Spain had sided with the colonies in the American Revolution. On September 3, 1783, the United States formally returned both Florida provinces to Spain. For a few years afterward, Spain's colonies formed an unbroken band from the Atlantic to the Pacific along the southern U.S. border. But within 38 years, these possessions would all be lost.

President Thomas Jefferson

It began with the purchase of Louisiana by **Thomas Jefferson** in 1803. The Spanish king had returned the vast territory to France in 1800 in a secret swap for land in Italy that never came to pass. So when the emperor of France, **Napoleon Bonaparte**, decided to sell Louisiana to Jefferson, there was nothing Spain could do.

The forts in Florida, meanwhile, had fallen into decay under British control. American frontiersmen had pushed across the borders and set up homesteads in West Florida. They began appealing to the United States for **annexation**, and in 1810 the United States took West Florida over the protests of Spain. On February 2, 1819, Spain signed a treaty that transferred all of La Florida to the United States.

For years, Spanish Americans had been developing an identity separate from Spaniards. In 1808, Napoleon Bonaparte seized Spain. He was removed in 1814, but during his short rule Spain's South American colonies began declaring their independence. On September 16, 1810, a friar named **Miguel Hidalgo y Costilla** and several hundred of his parishioners seized a prison at Dolores, Mexico, beginning Mexico's struggle for independence.

Fort at St. Augustine, Florida

A Texas town in the 1800s

The **Treaty of Córdoba** of 1821 gave Mexico its independence. In North America, provinces that had belonged to Spain—Alta California, New Mexico, and Texas—now were part of Mexico. The region was still very remote from its capital, which was now Mexico City. Thinly populated and weakly defended, it was ripe for takeover by the United States.

To help populate the empty plains, Spain had encouraged Americans to move into Texas. In 1820, **Moses Austin** had won permission to establish a colony of non-Hispanic Americans there. This changed Spain's earlier policies, under which foreigners were unwelcome in Spain's territories. By 1836 Texas had about 35,000 non-Hispanic colonists, outnumbering Hispanic people by about 10 to 1.

# THE ALAMO

In 1835 border **skirmishes** began between Texans and Mexicans trying to defend their missions around San Antonio. **Antonio López de Santa Anna**, a Mexican general, fought back. At Mission San Antonio—now renamed The Alamo—he found 187 men defending it. In an extremely bloody battle, all 187 were killed, including frontiersman **Davy Crockett**. But the Texans retaliated at the Battle of San Jacinto, capturing Santa Anna and forcing him to surrender. On May 14, 1836, the Republic of Texas was born.

Antonio López de Santa Anna (above).
The Alamo at night (below)

Texas declared independence from Mexico in 1837 and then spent eight years as the "Lone Star Republic." The Texans petitioned the United States for annexation, but a main obstacle was slavery. Anti-slavery Congressmen rejected early requests to annex Texas.

When Mexico became independent, foreigners were no longer discouraged. Mexico desired foreign trade, and soon wagon trains were common on the **Santa Fe Trail** between Missouri and Santa Fe. The province of Alta California also saw changes. Ship traffic greatly increased, with Boston traders bringing all kinds of goods in exchange for hides and **tallow**. Also, overland traffic to California grew on the **Spanish Trail** from Santa Fe and the **Oregon Trail** from Missouri.

Traveling one of the westward trails

On February 28, 1845, the U.S. Congress voted to invite Texas into the union. Mexico protested and broke off relations. In November, President **James K. Polk** attempted to buy New Mexico and California, but Mexico refused to negotiate. Texas became the 28th state of the United States on December 29, 1845.

General Zachary Taylor

In the spring of 1846 President Polk sent General **Zachary Taylor** with 4,000 troops to camp on the north bank of the Rio Grande, which was **disputed** territory. This provoked Mexican attacks, allowing Polk to declare war on Mexico. It is known as the Mexican War. In June, Polk sent a separate force, "The Army of the West," led by General **Stephen Watts Kearny**, to conquer New Mexico. Kearny and 1,500 troops entered Santa Fe and took it without a fight on August 16. By this time, California had also been taken.

Meanwhile, Taylor moved deeper into Mexico, pushing back Santa Anna. In March 1847, another general, **Winfield Scott**, landed 10,000 troops on Mexico's eastern coast. He took Veracruz and marched toward the capital, engaging in fierce battles along the way. On September 9, 1847, Scott occupied Mexico City.

Mexico signed the **Treaty of Guadalupe Hidalgo** on February 2, 1848. It ceded California, New Mexico, and what are now Arizona, Nevada, Utah, Wyoming, Colorado, and parts of Kansas and Oklahoma to the United States. Although Mexico received $15 million for these lands, she gave them up only to avoid losing everything.

General Scott rides into Mexico City, 1847.

Citizens of the formerly Mexican (and recently Spanish) provinces now found that they had become conquered peoples. Like Native Americans, they were soon treated as foreigners in many ways—even though the Treaty of Guadalupe Hidalgo had granted them all of the rights of citizens. After 300 years of developing a distinct culture and way of life, they were now subject to the Anglo-American's **prejudices** against darker-skinned people. Partly because of this prejudice, statehood for New Mexico and Arizona (two of the states formed out of Nuevo México) was delayed until 1912.

The Gadsden Purchase was signed in Mexico City (right).

## THE GADSDEN PURCHASE

In 1853, American foreign minister **James Gadsden** convinced Mexico to sell 30,000 square miles (77,700 sq km) of land in what is now southern Arizona and New Mexico. The United States wanted to build a railroad along this route. The **Gadsden Purchase** filled out the present shape of the **continental** United States along its southern edge.

Americans who came from England and northern Europe greatly outnumbered Hispanic Americans in Florida even before the Mexican War. A strong Hispanic presence remained, however, in Southern California, Arizona, Texas, and especially along the Rio Grande valley in New Mexico. As late as 1859, sessions of the New Mexico legislature were held in Spanish rather than English.

A parade celebrating Spanish history in New Mexico

As the United States grew in prosperity, large numbers of Hispanic people from Mexico migrated across the border to work in agriculture, railroad building, and other industries. As the years passed, Anglo-Americans lost their sense of which Hispanic people were native to the Southwest and which were recent immigrants from Mexico. In

Agricultural workers along the border of the United States and Mexico

addition, Spain had ceded one of its last colonies, Puerto Rico, to the United States after losing the Spanish-American War of 1898. By 1910, Puerto Ricans had begun migrating to the United States, mostly to New York, by the thousands.

The blending of all of the cultures that make up the United States, along with the unique contributions of each of those cultures, continues. The offerings that Spain has brought to America, beginning with Christopher Columbus in 1492, are among the richest threads in the intricate **tapestry** of U.S. history.

# A TIMELINE OF THE HISTORY OF
# The SPANISH in AMERICA

| | |
|---|---|
| **1492** | Christopher Columbus lands on an island in what is now the Bahamas. |
| **1513** | Juan Ponce de León sails along present-day United States coast, names the land "Pascua Florida" or La Florida, and claims it for Spain. |
| **1519-1521** | Hernán Cortés defeats the Aztec empire in what is now Mexico. |
| **1521** | Ponce de León attempts to establish a colony near Tampa Bay. |
| **1526** | Founding of San Miguel de Gualdape on Georgia/South Carolina coast. |
| **1528** | Narváez expedition lands near Tampa Bay, beginning the eight-year wanderings of Álvar Nuñez Cabeza de Vaca. |
| **1531** | Francisco Pizarro conquers the Inca empire in present-day Peru. |
| **1539** | Marcos de Niza expedition ends in death of Esteban, the black slave who accompanied Cabeza de Vaca. |
| **1539-1543** | De Soto expedition through what is now the southeastern United States. |
| **1540-1542** | Coronado expedition explores the present-day Southwest. |
| **1542-1543** | Juan Rodríguez Cabrillo's party explores Baja and Alta California. |
| **1565** | Pedro Menéndez de Avilés founds San Augustín. |
| **1598** | Juan Oñate y Salazar founds first permanent settlement in Nuevo México. |
| **1610** | Founding of Santa Fe, the oldest capital in the United States. |
| **1680** | Popé leads Pueblo Revolt, expelling Spaniards from Nuevo México for 13 years. |
| **1682** | Franciscans begin to build missions in what is now Texas. |
| **1692** | Diego de Vargas Zapata Luján y Ponce de León reconquers Nuevo México. |
| **1702** | England attacks San Augustín. |
| **1762-1800** | Spain controls the Louisiana Territory. |
| **1763** | End of the French and Indian War in which Spain cedes La Florida to England. |

| | |
|---|---|
| **1769** | King Carlos III sends José de Gálvez to inspect the colonies; he recommends building missions and presidios from San Diego to Monterey Bay in what is now California. |
| **1769** | Captain Gaspar de Portolá seeks overland supply trail to Monterey. Junípero Serra builds the first of 21 Alta California missions at San Diego. |
| **1774-1775** | Captain Juan Bautista de Anza finds overland supply route from Sonora to the California coast and brings first settlers to Monterey and San Francisco. |
| **1776-1783** | The American Revolution gains independence for the English colonies, creating the United States of America. Florida is returned to Spain in 1783. |
| **1777** | Monterey is named the capital of New California. |
| **1781** | The Yuma people close the Colorado River crossing to Spaniards. |
| **1803** | President Thomas Jefferson purchases Louisiana Territory from France. |
| **1808-1814** | Napoleon Bonaparte is emperor of Spain; South American colonies begin to break free. |
| **1810** | The United States takes West Florida over Spain's protests. Mexico begins its struggle for independence. |
| **1819** | The United States buys all of Florida from Spain. |
| **1821** | Mexico wins independence from Spain; former Spanish colonies are now under Mexico. |
| **1835** | Battle of The Alamo in San Antonio, Texas. |
| **1837-1845** | Texas declares independence from Mexico and exists as the "Lone Star Republic," becoming a U.S. state in 1845. |
| **1846** | President Polk sends General Zachary Taylor to the Rio Grande, triggering the Mexican War. |
| **1847** | The United States occupies Mexico City, forcing Mexico to surrender. |
| **1848** | The Treaty of Guadalupe Hidalgo transfers Nuevo México and California to the United States. |
| **1853** | In the Gadsden Purchase, Mexico sells the United States additional land along the southern border of New Mexico and Arizona. |

# GLOSSARY

**adelantado** - A title that gave a Spanish subject the right to conquer an unconquered territory.

**Alta California** - "Upper California," the northern segment of "California," now the U.S. state by that name.

**annexation** - Attachment of something, such as a territory, to something larger, such as a state or country.

**Apache** - A native group of the American Southwest speaking an Athabascan language.

**Arawak** - The natives of Hispaniola, destroyed by Columbus.

**Aztec** - A native civilization that rose to power in Mexico's central valley around 1450.

**Baja California** - "Lower California," or the southern segment of "California," a peninsula in western Mexico.

**barter** - To trade by exchanging wares rather than money.

**buffer** - A device used as a cushion against damage or shock.

**Cofitachequi** - Muskogean-speaking Natives in what is now South Carolina, now extinct.

**colonist** - A person who establishes a colony.

**colonize** - To establish a colony or settle a new land or region.

**Comanche** - A Native American group that roamed over the Great Plains and the Southwest, and spoke a Uto-Aztecan language.

**conquistador** - Spanish for "conqueror"; a leader in the Spanish conquest of America.

**continental** - Relating to a continent, one of the great divisions of land on the globe.

**conversion** - The bringing about of a change in a person's beliefs.

**convert** - To convince a person to change beliefs; a person who has been brought over from one belief to another.

**Coosa** - A Muskogean-speaking Native group, now extinct, of South Carolina.

**criollo** - A person of pure Spanish descent born in America.

**disputed** - Not agreed upon.

**domain** - Territory over which a claim of ownership is exercised.

**drought** - A prolonged period of dryness.

**emerald** - A rich green gemstone.

**fanfare** - A showy display, especially involving a lively sounding of trumpets.

**fortress** - Stronghold; large fortification.

**Franciscan** - The Order of Friars Minor established by St. Francis of Assisi in 1209.

**French and Indian War** (1756-1763) - A worldwide conflict growing out of the competition between France and England for an overseas empire.

**friar** - A member of a religious order dedicated to poverty and engaging in religious activity.

**Gadsden Purchase** - A 30,000-acre (77,700-sq km) tract of land in present-day southern Arizona and New Mexico purchased in 1853 from Mexico.

**Gulf of Mexico** - The portion of the Atlantic Ocean that extends along the southern edge of the United States and the eastern edge of Mexico.

**Hispaniola** - The first Spanish colony in the New World, which Columbus named "Española" ("Spanish woman").

**immunity** - The ability to resist a particular disease.

**Inca** - Native group of today's Peru that formed an empire from about 1250 to 1500.

**Manso** - Spanish for "tame," a name given to the natives of the region of what is now El Paso, Texas.

**maraud** - To roam about and raid in search of goods to steal.

**measles** - A contagious disease caused by a virus, marked by an eruption of red, circular spots.

**mestizo** - A person of mixed European and Native American ancestry.

**ministry** - The functions of a minister, or one who directs church worship; a group of such ministers.

**missionary** - A person undertaking a mission, especially a religious mission.

**Native American** - A member of the first peoples of North America.

**nomadic** - Roaming about from place to place; migrating with the seasons.

**Nueva España** - "New Spain," in Spanish, a name the conquistadors gave to what is now Mexico.

**Oregon Trail** - The route from Independence, Missouri, to the Northwest and California, beginning in the 1830s.

**pacify** - To restore to a peaceful state.

**Pecos** - One of the larger New Mexico pueblos; now an abandoned archeological site and national monument.

**Pope** - The head of the Roman Catholic Church, whose headquarters is Vatican City in Rome.

**prejudice** - Injury resulting from a decision or action that affects one's rights.

**presidio** - A military post or fortified settlement.

**pueblo** - Spanish for "people" or "village"; name given to non-nomadic Native American groups in New Mexico.

**requerimiento** - A required speech that conquistadors gave to Native American peoples in seeking to conquer and dominate them.

**Roanoke** - Settlement attempt by Sir Walter Raleigh on an island off present-day North Carolina.

**Roman Catholic** - A Christian church with priests and bishops under the authority of a pope.

**San Agustín** - The first permanent settlement by Europeans in what is now the United States.

**San Miguel de Gualdape** - The name of a short-lived Spanish settlement on the east coast of what is now the United States.

**Santa Fe Trail** - Wagon trail from Independence, Missouri, to Santa Fe, New Mexico, used from about 1820 to 1850.

**scurvy** - A disease caused by the lack of Vitamin C.

**sect** - A subgroup of a religion.

**Seven Cities of Cíbola** - Legendary place in the Southwest that Native Americans had told Spaniards was full of treasure.

**skirmish** - A minor fight or a minor battle in a larger war.

**smallpox** - A contagious disease marked by fever and skin eruptions.

**Spanish Trail** - Also known as "Old Spanish Trail," a trading route from Santa Fe, New Mexico, to Los Angeles, California.

**successor** - One who follows, especially in assuming a throne, title, estate, or office.

**tallow** - The white, solid fat of cattle or sheep, which is processed and used in candles and soap.

**tapestry** - A heavy hand-woven textile or something resembling it in richness and complexity.

**Tascaloosa** - A native group of Alabama, now extinct.

**Treaty of Córdoba** - Treaty between Spain and Mexico in 1821, giving Mexico its independence.

**Treaty of Guadalupe Hidalgo** - Treaty signed by Mexico and the United States, in which Mexico gave up New Mexico, California, and the territory between them and north of them.

**turquoise** - A mineral that is blue, blue-green, or greenish gray, containing copper and aluminum.

**typhoid** - An infectious disease marked by fever and diarrhea.

**typhus** - A group of bacteria-caused diseases marked by fever and a red rash.

**viceroy** - The governor of a country or province who rules as a king's representative.

**West Indies** - The islands between southeastern North America and northern South America, bordering the Caribbean Sea.

**Zuni** - A major tribe of Pueblo Native Americans in New Mexico.

46

**Anza, Juan Bautista de** (1736-1788) - Governor of New Mexico (1778-1787) and Spanish-American pioneer who opened a supply route from the province of Sonora to the California missions (1775-1776).

**Austin, Moses** (1761-1821) - U.S. pioneer who settled the first American families in Texas.

**Bonaparte, Napoleon** (1769-1821) - French Army officer who seized power after the French Revolution and in 1804 named himself emperor.

**Cabeza de Vaca, Álvar Nuñez** (c. 1490-c. 1557) - Spanish explorer who was shipwrecked off the Texas coast and was one of the first Europeans to explore the American Southwest.

**Cabrillo, Juan Rodríguez** (died 1543) - Portuguese explorer in the service of Spain; European discoverer of California (1542).

**Carlos III** (1716-1788) - King of Spain (1759-1788).

**Columbus, Christopher** (1451-1506) - Italian explorer in the service of Spain who discovered America for the Europeans in 1492.

**Coronado, Francisco Vásquez de** (c. 1510-1554) - Spanish explorer who traveled through the American Southwest (1540-1542).

**Cortés, Hernán** (1485-1547) - Central figure in the Spanish conquest and colonization of Mexico.

**Crockett, Davy** (1786-1836) - U.S. frontiersman from Tennessee.

**De Soto y Gutiérrez Cardeñosa, Hernando Méndez** (c. 1500-1542) - Spanish adventurer who explored what is now the southeastern United States (1539-1542).

**Drake, Francis** (1540-1596) - English sailor and adventurer who raided Spanish ships and colonies in the Caribbean.

**Esteban** (1500?-1539) - African slave who guided Spanish explorers Nárvaez and Cabeza de Vaca (1528-1536) and later Marcos de Niza into the Southwest.

**Felipe II** (Philip II, 1527-1598) - King of Spain (1556-96).

**Felipe III** (Philip III, 1578-1621) - King of Spain (1598-1621), son of Philip II.

**Gadsden, James** (1788-1858) - American minister to Mexico who negotiated the Gadsden Purchase in 1853-1854.

**Gálvez, José de** (1729-1786) - Spanish politician named as general inspector of the American colonies in 1765.

**Hidalgo y Costilla, Miguel** (1753-1811) - Mexican priest and leader of the country's independence movement.

**Jefferson, Thomas** (1743-1826) - Third president of the United States (1801-1809).

**Kearny, Stephen Watts** (1774-1848) - U.S. general who took possession of New Mexico in 1846.

**Marcos de Niza** (c. 1495-1558) - Franciscan friar who led an exploration of the American Southwest in 1539 in advance of Coronado.

**Mendoza, Antonio de** (1490-1552) - First viceroy of Nueva España (1535 to 1550).

**Menendez de Aviles, Pedro** (1519-1574) - Spanish explorer who established the settlement of St. Augustine, Florida (1565). He became Florida's first Spanish governor.

**Narváez, Pánfilo de** (c. 1470-1528) - Spanish conquistador who was commissioned by Carlos V to conquer Florida and was lost at sea.

**Oñate y Salazar, Juan** (c. 1549-c. 1624) - Spanish explorer who established the first settlement in Nuevo México (1598).

**Peralta, Pedro de** (1584-1666) - Governor of Nuevo México following Oñate.

**Pizarro, Francisco** (c. 1471-1541) - Leader of the Spanish conquest of Peru (1530-1535).

**Polk, James K.** (1795-1849) - The 11th president of the United States (1845-1849).

**Ponce de León, Juan** (1460?-1521) - Spanish explorer who traveled with Columbus on his second voyage and explored the Florida coast (1513).

**Popé** - San Juan native who led the successful Pueblo Revolt against the Spanish in 1680.

**Portolá, Gaspar de** (1734-1784) - Spanish governor of Baja California who discovered San Francisco Bay.

**Santa Anna, Antonio López de** (1794-1876) - Mexican general who was defeated by General Winfield Scott in the Mexican War (1846-1848); president of Mexico on several occasions.

**Scott, Winfield** (1786-1866) - U.S. military officer from Virginia who led the march from Veracruz to Mexico City during the Mexican War (1846-1848).

**Serra, Junípero** (1713-1784) - Franciscan missionary from Mallorca, who began the chain of missions in California (1769-1784).

**Taylor, Zachary** (1784-1850) - Twelfth president of the United States (1849-1850); general who led U.S. troops in the Mexican War (1846-1848).

**Vargas Zapata Luján y Ponce de León, Diego de** (c. 1643-1704) - Spaniard who led the reconquest of Nuevo México in 1693.

**Vásquez de Ayllón, Lucas** (c. 1480-1526) - Spanish lawyer who founded San Miguel de Gualdape in 1526, the first European settlement in what is now the United States.

# INDEX

## Books of Interest

Collier, Christopher and James Collier. *Hispanic America, Texas, and the Mexican War 1835-1850*, Benchmark Books, 1998.

Favor, Lesli J. *Francisco Vasquez de Coronado: Famous Journeys to the American Southwest and Colonial New Mexico*, Rosen Publishing Group, 2003.

Garland, Sherry. *A Line in the Sand: The Alamo Diary of Lucinda Lawrence, Gonzales, Texas, 1836 (Dear America)*, Scholastic, 1998.

Kalman, Bobbie and Greg Nickles. *Spanish Missions*, Crabtree Publishing Company, 1996.

Stein, R. Conrad. *In the Spanish West (How We Lived)*, Benchmark Books, 1999.

Waldman, Stuart and Tom McNeely. *We Asked for Nothing: The Remarkable Journey of Cabeza de Vaca*, Mikaya Press, 2003.

Weber, Valerie J. and Dale Anderson. *The California Missions (Events That Shaped America)*, Gareth Stevens Publishing, 2002.

Williams, Jack S. and Thomas L. Davis. *Indians of the California Mission (People of the California Missions)*, The Rosen Publishing Group's PowerKids Press, 2004.

## Web Sites of Interest

http://www.ecb.org/tracks/mod2.htm

http://www.u-s-history.com/pages/h438.html

http://www.pbs.org/weta/thewest/resources/archives/one/cabeza.htm

http://anza.uoregon.edu/

http://www.pbs.org/weta/thewest/people/s_z/serra.htm

Linda Thompson is a Montana native and a graduate of the University of Washington. She was a teacher, writer, and editor in the San Francisco Bay Area for 30 years and now lives in Taos, New Mexico. She can be contacted through her web site,

http://www.highmesaproductions.com